labyrinth soul

daelynn e.d. huber

Selah Press

Published by Selah Press
SelahPress.com

Cover design art by Daelynn E. D. Huber

ISBN: 978-0-9967428-2-5

labyrinth — soul

*for the ones who inspired it all, the ones who loved me,
and the ones who have never left my side.*
-dedh

01

there's poetry
hidden inside you
locked away in
your labyrinth soul
and i don't know
if you ever learned
to let it out

it can hurt
it can hurt more than anything
it can be so painful
to put pen to paper
and bare your soul
but oh
my darling
words
glint
just behind
your tired eyes
and they're words
of hope
of love
of healing;

let them whisper
let them flow
let them ache if they must
but do not ever
stifle
your soul

02

child
the light is rising

this darkness can't last
much longer
you say
you're all alone
but you just can't see
through this twilight
you can't see
my hand reaching out for yours

i'm here for you
and i won't leave

the light is rising
the dawn is breaking
and i've been here all along

come on
you're strong

you've held your ground
and now it's time
to let go
of all
you've been holding on to

that burden isn't good for you
so stand up straight
and let it hit the ground
because you don't need
to bear it anymore
i'm right here next to you
i'm not leaving

come on
look around
this life won't let you
stop for breath

so get back on your feet
let your heart breathe out
all the love i know
you have inside
you have power
in your soul
you've just got to
let it all spill out

the light is rising
the dawn is breaking
reality is rough
i know
but you are so so strong
and you are not alone

come on

03

some things
you cannot rationalize

sometimes
you cannot dull the pain
with facts
and reasons
and logic
and

sometimes
it takes
more than words
to heal a wound

more than a poem
to help your soul

and some things cannot
be endured
with advice
or aid
or someone's help

sometimes there is more
to pain
than just knowing how
or why
sometimes you just have to
let it hurt
for a little while
before it heals

04

don't loom over me like that
your shadow makes me
nervous

like before i step
on stage

sit down
have tea
i don't care for silence

05

i write the same
poem
over and over
a different pile
of half-wasted words
crumbling
at my feet
        and
until i find
the combination that
i crave
that broken jumble
of heartache
and salt water
is only
going
to grow

06

we carved our names
into the trees
trying to leave a mark
that the world would remember
but the trees grew
and the letters faded
and one day
they'll be gone again

07

twist and turn
curves of millions
a dance between two souls
take me away
and twist and turn
with the highway song
trees looming overhead
like friendly giants
shadow the way
follow the light
past the woods
eventually

08

i am tired of being tired
of being achy
and in pain
i'm tired of hiding behind
the fear
that i'm not good enough
i'm tired of feeling
that no matter what
i do
no matter how hard i try
things pile up and
things drag me down

earth is heavier than i thought
and the weight
of responsibility is
dragging me down
a lot faster than i
ever thought it would

sometimes i think it's easier
to just say
i'm depressed
rather than to truly
search my soul
for what is wrong

maybe it's because
the self examination that
hurts like heaven and earth
are breaking apart
is not really the problem
and as humans
we hate pain
but i want
to be something other than
mundane

09

keep on loving
love when you feel like
less than nothing
love when you feel
too weak to stand up straight
love when your heart
is cracking from the pressure
love when you're
empty and tired
love when your mind
is in utter chaos
just love

10

sleep calls again
the numbness
of dying to it all
is growing once more

my eyes close

i try in vain
to stay awake

every breath i take
is slow and weak

the world is tugging me
to sleep
to rest

to drift without a thought

to wander

aimlessly
and i follow

numbly

but i hear
a voice
a strong
calm voice
calling out to me

my eyelids stir
my mind turns again
i shake my sleeping limbs
and
hands lift me
from the realm of dreams

"please don't let me
fall asleep "
i whisper to Him

11

there'll be days that feel like fire
and days that feel like rain

your eyes will shine like silver
a song will fill your veins

a memory will hold you close
until your soul is stained

a voice will whisper softly
through the darkness of your pain

12

there's a lot
in this life
that will ache

that will cut
to the heart
in a moment

when the moment
seems perfect
and ends
and kills

13

sometimes i feel
so insanely happy
that i think i'll stop breathing
and it's not
for any particular reason
at least for me

i can be doing nothing
laundry
cleaning
hugging
and joy
intense as the sea
fills my soul

and those are the moments
when i'm happy
to be
alive

14

maybe someday
we will learn to silence the fears
that bind us
we will learn to love the pain
that shapes us
we will learn to brave the storm
that rocks us
but until then our hearts will be
l o u d
and until then we will try to
b r e a t h e
and until then we will try to be
s t r o n g

15

i wish my heart
didn't get attached
quite so easily
because maybe now
it would be simpler to go back
to the way things were
before i changed

16

love is so very hard
you get broken
and bruised
and you have to let
it damage you

you have to clamber
through all the
fear and doubt
and pain

for if its worth anything at all
you'll fight
and hurt and
rage
and come out
stronger

and maybe a bit softer
and wiser
in the end

17

maybe i'm searching
in the wrong way
for the wrong thing

and maybe i need too much
and love too hard
for things i can never
even have

maybe without you
i'll feel alone

but maybe i'll find
someone
who will be as fond of me
as i wanted you to be

and maybe i'll find someone
who talks to me about
the deepest things
inside his soul

18

people
are two souls

one is the noonday soul
the one of politeness
friendliness
happiness

the other is the midnight soul
and that one is the wild one
the careless one
the radiant one

when they
are tired enough that
emotional barriers break down
and there is no awkwardness
or hurt

and everything is far more simple
in the dark
than in the daylight

19

you said
to write

i told you
i'd written out
all the chaos

and now all i'm left with
is inky confusion
and

an echoing heart

20

there was an
anthem
that i heard
when i was lost
among the souls of men
a song so strong
so pure and true
an echo
of something greater
than anything i could
see
a song of hope
of life
of love
of dreams and prayers
both lost and lived
somehow that song
pierced me
and i lifted my voice
to join in the harmony

21

there is tired
behind your eyes
hiding just beyond
the light

what weighs your soul
my love?

what aches
do you carry
within you?

your hands were not meant
to bear the world
your legs were not formed
to be broken by care
your love was not created
to be diminished

22

i wish i could mend your heart
the one that aches from breaking

i wish i could stop your tears
the ones coursing down your cheeks

i wish i could protect you
the one with all the fears

23

there is pain
that refuses to leave
me alone
it clings to my back
between my shoulder blades
and it aches
and bleeds
and hurts
there was hope
that resisted
evacuation
and it still hides
trembling
in my rib cage
beside my heart
and it loves
and loves
and loves

24

it's an old house
overgrown in vines and folly

try not to get lost

wind your way through
forgotten gardens
until you find the door

footsteps
raise the dust
and it clings to the tip of your boot
don't stop to brush it
away
but keep on searching
until you are
Home

25

i was fire
when i was born
and you
were the water
that doused me

when i was young
i was an ocean of mystery
and you
you were the moon
pulling me out
into oblivion
until i fit what you wanted

when i was a teenager
i was a mirror
cracked
but not
shattered
and you held a sledgehammer
forgotten
by your side
when i'm old
i hope i'm a tree
with roots that grow
deep and strong
and i pray

i pray

i pray

you won't be the lightning
that brings me down

// people hurt people

26

you can touch your scars
you can point them out
and tell how each one
became a part of you

you can run your fingers
over the marks left
from a lifetime of pain
and hope
but it's the scars you cannot touch
that haunt you

it's the ones you can't describe
or wonder at
that hurt you the deepest

it's the scars
on your heart
that you feel the clearest

the ones in your soul
that matter the most

27

i'm the middle of the night
i'm the whisper no one hears
i'm the dream that you forget
i'm the song you've always feared
i'm the heart no one can see
i'm the wish that no one made
i'm the letter never written
i'm the lesson never learned
i'm the love without a hope
i'm a cry without a voice
i'm the one you used to care for
but all that's disappeared

28

Don't you dare make me forget
Don't you dare let me miss you
Don't you dare let me regret

29

shopping list

rubber boots to wade through salty tears

an umbrella to keep off any emotional downpour

glasses to see the truth through dreams and hopes

pomegranates because they taste delicious and my
soul needs the taste

a drawer full of dreams to inspire my heart again

a box of watercolors to paint my mind brighter

earbuds to shut out this lonely world with music

bandaids to cover the cuts in other people's souls

30

we're all
just clinging
to the people
we have memorized
scared
that one day
they'll slip out of reach
and become someone new
and we'll be
left alone
taking up
the same static
space

31

every time i sing
i hear
your voice echo
after mine
and somehow
though it's through
murky time
from somewhere i've never been
i know it's your heart calling
out to me

i'm coming
it says
wait for me
until i find you

i can hear mine answer
hurry my love
for the days
loom long and dark ahead
of me
and i don't know how i'll be
able to face them
and i'm not quite sure how
i will cope
without you
by my side

32

i am everything i used to be
but every breath i take
my heart beats a little quicker
a little odder
and every step i take
i grow a little stronger
a little wiser
and every word i speak
i'm a little more who i'm supposed to be
a little stranger
a little more me

33

you told me i was worthy
of all the love in the world
you told me i deserved the sky
you told me to follow my heart
for surely my heart knows best
you told me i had all i needed inside me

you lied to me

i'm a mess
some say i shouldn't say that
but it's my truth
i'm a mess
and if i'm not
i should be
i'm not a perfect picture of happiness
but a snapshot of depravity
i'm a failure
i'm unworthy
i'm ugly
i'm useless
i'm nothing

until Him
when Light touched my life
oh how things changed

when weakness drew me to Him
He reached down and gave me strength
to stand again
when i lay before Him
worthless and pointless
He gave grace and love and
stretched out His hand to me
when i say i am a mess
it's because without Him
i'm a mess
and i need Someone to clean me up
i'm a mess
and i can rejoice because if i wasn't
tangled and broken
there wouldn't be any reason
to need Him

34

i'm a silhouette of forgetfulness
lost in an eddy
of feathery memories

nearly ruptured
by fragments of clarity

each breath is agony
for my heart is unrelenting

it is ceaselessly searching
for the calm

35

you seem alone
and sad
but when you smile
it's the most
beautiful thing
i have ever seen

36

you lose people
and you find them again
you meet someone
who brightens your life
for a day or two
who gives you joy
and happiness
who intoxicates you
and then you leave

or they leave
without a second glance
for memories
and all you have left
is a mind full of people
you may never see again

how do you
cope with the fact
that those
few memories are all
you might ever have?

how do you
erase someone from
your heart
who never had their
proper chance
to grow?
how do you
live with them
inside your head
taking up every corner
when all you want
is to never be torn from them
again

but you know that the chances
of that happening
are like zero to
a zillion

and you know
sensibly
that they'll move on
forget you maybe
and you'll never see them
again

but i still hold hope
in my heart
that one day i'll see
them again
or learn to live
with/out them

37

i once thought
it would be hard
to show a human
part of my soul
a part that i'd hidden
and i was right

it hurts like crazy
but it hurts a whole lot more
to keep it to myself

38

i wish i could write
all the things i feel
or how empty my soul
can be

people ache and burn
darkness settles
and i don't want it
to settle on me

all my life
i wanted to be more
to be something i'm not
and i never realized
until now
that i am
what i am

i am bold
i am strong
i am light
in Him

without Him
i am darkness
but just because
i'm in the dark right now
doesn't mean i have to
stay here

the darkness may try
to drag me down
but light's gonna prevail
it will strike my eyes
until i can't breathe
and the dark recedes

39

when my tears stopped
the rain was gone
leaving a hole
in my heart
big enough to die in
and when i left
i only wanted to stay
for i was safe there
and i was loved
and i had hope

40

i wander outside
away from the soul draining
futilities of life
and i let my feet
cross the meadow

they've memorized
the way
the path tread by those
who have come before

the wind dances
tugging at my messy hair
and together they twirl and leap

my eyes catch sight of my home

i've come full circle
yet again

41

i speak
but instead of
speaking from my
soul

from my heart

i let fear sway me
and i avoid

any confusion
any oddities
any weirdness
any unusual concepts
any queer hopes
any misunderstandings
any foolish arguments
any words that set me apart
as different

and i only
speak what
people
want to hear

42

i'm still learning
wonder
flows through my veins
and starlight
stuns my eyes

i'm still learning
to sway
in the wind

when storms
rise against me

i'm still learning
to dance
when my legs are aching

i'm still learning

43

mist is flowing
from beneath my bed
again
carrying faint wisps
of tears cried
over years
of pain

44

into your hands
i placed
pieces of my soul
for you to read
and learn
and maybe even love

and you

you accepted them with grace
and peace

and only i knew the weight
of the gift you had given me

the gift of seeing
and accepting

of watching
and remembering

of listening
and understanding

// for the ones who listened and loved

45

the light fades
from your eyes
i can see childhood
ebbing away from your soul
but don't let go
cling tight
cling tight
cling tight
for the love you have now
is lifeblood
in an otherwise
dreary world

46

even if my heart wasn't already
a tangled mess
i think you'd create
chaos in my soul
without even trying

craziness is in my bloodstream
and my heartbeat is going haywire
unintentionally i'm changing
to someone i didn't used to be
someone i don't want to be
someone who scares me
someone who isn't me
and my head is going crazy with all
those great big wondrous dreams of mine
and half of them involve you you know
cause i don't take things slow
and every blink i wish i'd see you
because
my heart is a tangled mess

47

i used to think
that hope
was a roaring song
now i know
it's a heartbeat

48

do i really care if
someone knows
anything about my soul
or any small tidbits of
my heart?

do i really care if i hide
myself from all
the prying eyes
or if no one really truly
knows me?

is my heart a place
to share
or should i keep it safe?

is my heart
sacred to myself?

cause i'm scared that
if i show anyone
they won't realize
it's importance
that they'll trample it unknowingly

somehow to me
it seems that every
time i want to heal
to show my secrets to a
soul i love

they don't ever care

i think that small talk
is hiding
behind a mask
and keeping my own heart
safe

so give me pain
and freedom
and give me
the breath of life

do not give me
empty words
but instead give me
words that ache
and jerk with pain
and ones that hold
me captive
and give me those you've kept inside
away from all the dust of time
and show me what you
do not love

i'll love it for you
and i'll never let you go

49

my favorite shirt has a hole
in the sleeve
near the elbow

and i would be lying
if i said
i didn't shed a few tears
today

but they weren't
brought on by a rip

50

sometimes
i'm scared of the dark

i'm frightened that
something will reach
out and catch my ankle

i know it's silly
but i wish you
were here beside me
to hold my hand
and to comfort me

when the night
is too dark
for me

51

my heart is not
a complacent place

it rails against
the dying embers
of any dream
that seized it

a heart like mine
is hard to live with
for each breath i take
longs for something else

my heart is loud
and it's loud for love
for hope
for joy
and i hope that
i can turn the loudness
from that fear
into a new dream

52

i was lost
in a stormy sea
in a raging gale

the sea echoed
the color of your eyes

i was tossed to and fro
and the waves crashed over me
dashing me against
the rocks of despair

save me from
myself
before i destroy
all i've ever wanted

// i don't want to lose you

53

sitting cross legged

thinking deep
into the cold unblinking
night

of every echo
i once held
between my fingers

my bones
are stretching
aching
elongating

and growing pains
hurt like
ice in my veins

go away
i say

never letting go
of the remaining
weight
that still calls
my name

54

i feel like love
is shaky

how can you know
if someone truly loves you
or if you only hope they do
or if you love someone else's soul?

i feel like love
hurts

really hurts

it damages you
changes you
morphs you into something else

you can hurt
you can break
you can dream of love
but it may be a love you'll never get

i cannot tell if
it's better to love and
risk getting hurt
or stay safe
sequestered in your heart

55

it hurts

there's a pain in my chest
cause i feel so torn
so caught
tied between too many places

my heart will be ripped in pieces soon
because there's a piece of me
that's already
too attached to you
to let go without a bruise

and my hands have forgotten how to
let go
of things i cannot have

56

if one day
i can sing forever
sing praises to my Lord
if one day i can sit at
his glorious feet
if one day
i can live with Him
and never feel pain
that one thought
makes everything that hurts
fly away
the weight is
lifted
and i'm free again
knowing He has prepared
a place for me
a place reserved
held
never given away

and the most amazing fact of all
is
He loves
me

57

how did it happen?
one day you're a little kid
playing in the sand
whispering prayers at the foot of your bed
small enough to be scooped up in
your grandma's arms
and life's ahead of you

and then

suddenly you're seventeen
and you're finishing school
and you meet someone
and that someone
without ever trying
finds the hole in your heart

people say that love fills that hole
but for you
someone just
tears it more
and rips it apart
and they never even knew
they were hurting you
it wasn't their fault

it was circumstances

life

it was time

it just took someone away from you
too soon
and time heals all wounds
but does it heal the ones
it wounds?

58

dreams are filmed in turquoise
filed with the moon

hearts are stretching
yearning
reaching for the sky
for all the sinking ships
for all the damaged hands
trying to grasp the stars;

dreams of helping
people lost at sea
set aside with the lore
of elves and mer creatures
and held alongside
the blinking fears
waiting to stir
again

59

in the middle of the night
things that were once complex
simply drift
into place and
everything feels
right once more

60

"these words aren't ready"
i whispered
but i wrote them anyway
ripping them from the back of my throat
until it bled ink

maybe if i tear my heart out
it could heal

the problem is
i don't have tragedies
i don't have torture
i don't have abuse or hatred

i just have a little pain inside me
some fear and lies
that sing to me like lullabies
at night

maybe if i named my brain
he'd somehow be alright again

cause when you name something
it's able to hold on
and maybe that's just what he needs

[a hand to hold]
so he knows he's not alone

[a voice in the dark]
to call him to the light

[a dream to recall]
for when he's falling apart

61

i'm glad that we both exist
it makes me happy
to know that somewhere
you are breathing
you are dreaming
you are alive
and i never want it
any other way

62

my brothers laugh
joy spilling over
from their lungs
and my sister and i
plunge our heads
into cold water
because the heat
is so oppressing
and sunday afternoons
are made of
sunlight
and pound cake
and things that i will
one day
forget

63

you're me
i only just saw that

i only just noticed the lashes
that i've never seen blink
are a reflection of mine
and i only realized a moment ago that
each breath you take
i can feel my lungs expand
and i only just found out that
every time my heart breaks

there's a mirror image crack
in yours

64

when the rain stops
the clouds will part
and there will be color
in the world again

when the rain stops
my heart will have
a hole in it
that is a little bit
smaller than it used to be

when the rain stops
my hurt won't be
gone completely
but it might be a little bit
less painful

when the rain stops
my tears might end
or keep on flowing
and i might begin again
or i might not

when the rain stops
i'll make a choice
but while the rain pours
i'm caught in blissful
indecision
limbo

when the rain stops
i'll wake up
and i'll be me
but i'll be gone
and i'll not be the same

65

i like being called
pretty
lovely
beautiful

but that's only surface level

call me lovely
but also call me kind

call me pretty
but not just pretty

call me understanding
intriguing

call me strong
and brave
and honest
and intelligent

call me beautiful
but not because
my face is okay
call me beautiful
when i'm alive
and vibrant
and laughing
and crying
because beauty doesn't just come
from my skin

66

sure i'm a woman
sure i look nice sometimes
sure i can be kind

what do you know?
how do you look at me
and see only a body?

i am grace
and strength
and bravery

i am honor
and loyalty

i am love
and peace
and wisdom

i am a woman

67

there's a glint of light
shining through my window

like a speck of hoping
glowing
in a dark world

and i remember
trying to catch a sunbeam
but i could never hold it

i curl up on the floor
filling the space

the light flows over
and i let it seep
into my soul
and i'm at peace

you are the light
gleaming shimmering
before me

a spark of light
in the ocean of my mind

and you are the hope
that stirs within me

and you are the memory
of hope
that calms my weary fears

you are the spark
in the window

68

smoke from the ground
echoes in the sky
austere wisps shroud the sun
and love burns away
like the world we know

tall boots cradle calves
and ties encase necks
but we are falling apart at the seams

minstrels' voices fade
anxiety sets in

is hope lost like childhood
memories in the mind of a grown up?
pestered by a need for more
we're never content
until we've lost it all

69

i have an ache
for something i have
never known

an itch in my soul
for a distant land

a hole in my heart
for faces that are
strangers
that will one day
be family
and i wish
that time were
a catapult to where
you wanted to be

so you could skip the pain
the heartache
the headache
and find yourself
in joyful peace
with people you love
so very dearly
but without the pain the
laughter
grins
hugs
kisses

all the happiness you have now
would slip away

for from darkness
pours light

and from breaking
comes healing

and from heartache
grows love once more

70

my thoughts
don't flow so easily
t o d a y

my mind is lost in thought
my thoughts lost in translation
from my brain
to my voice
and my heart is lost in memories

i cannot form a sentence
to say why i'm hurting
why i'm hiding

i know there's no big cause
no one reason

just a fear in my head

and a terror in my heart
that i'm apprehensive to voice

even to you

71

grey walls
close in
around me
and i cannot breathe

the walls are drowned
in curse words and
tearstained prayers
moments of past fears
and bouts of insanity

the walls recede
when panic fades
but what if one day
they crush me

blood spilled

i fear
that one day
i won't be
strong enough
to hold them back
but until that day

i pray i'll stand strong
against the walls of my mind

72

i don't know
what you think about at 2 am
or how you look
at yourself in the mirror
or how you glance behind each memory
to see if you've changed

i don't know if
you look at me
the way i look at you
when your back is turned

i don't know
what songs you listen to
when you're all alone
i don't know what
brings tears to your eyes

but i'll bet you my life
and my heart
and my dreams
that i can love you
anyway

73

all this weight is dragging you down
and making you forget
who you really are

each breath you take is
flavored with destiny
and your heartbeat
somehow echoed mine

so let all that weight slide from
your fingertips
release the pain and all the hard things
you've been holding onto

for there's light
inside of you
and you can let it out through
your cracks and your brokenness

and maybe you can heal your broken heart
with the light that pours
from your soul

74

sometimes my heart
gets too heavy
weighed down by

memories that haunt my mind

loves that never had
the chance to start

dreams that died
before they flew

things i said
that made no sense
that hurt someone badly

stuff i can't
forgive myself for

i wish that i
could change the past
but life is
unchangeable
untraceable
unbelievable
unerasable

i'm living life
petrified of messing up
terrified of memories
much too scared to even dream
so i'm missing out
on good and bad
life is stifled
void of air and love
the things that make life life

the God of the universe
didn't create me for
regret
or fear
or worry
but for joy
hope
faith

75

as you drive
into the darkness
into the clouds
without the light
as you dream--

your eyes wide open--

waiting for a sign
as you wait
with hands prepared
to catch your fate

maybe tune your thoughts
to what you love
and what you
really care about

and maybe that will make the
darkness fade a little bit
and maybe that will
help the cracks in your heart
to heal a little more

and maybe

that's when you truly
understand

76

my soul is
a wildfire
consuming
burning
destroying

my heart is
a wanderer
incessantly
searching for the fullness
it felt when it
was younger

my eyes are
constellations
lost in the starry dreams
i once held inside me

my arms are
crossbows
attempting to shoot
love
into the souls
of every human
within reach

my lips are
raindrops
that try to fill
the void
left by
pain
and pain
and pain

my hands are broken
remnants of every
tear
scream
heart
and dream
i tried to hold
onto

77

my favorite clothes
slowly start to tear
first my flannel shirt
with the hole
in the elbow
next my comfy jeans
with a rip in the knee
maybe next will be
my hopes and dream
those scary
silhouettes

78

if i told you
not to worry
i think you'd
stress out anyway
because honestly
my words aren't
powerful enough
to change
anything
and i'm so relieved
for if my words
held that much power
inside of them
i could ruin you
and

—heaven knows—

that would
kill
me

79

i don't doubt
Your plans

i doubt mine

the ones that
crumble to pieces
at the slightest testing

i don't doubt
Your paths

just the one
i formed on my own
that twists off
into the wilderness

i don't doubt
that You hold me
i just doubt
my own perseverance
my worthiness
my beauty
my strength
my kindness
i doubt myself
not You

i doubt my humanity
will let You in

i doubt my legs
can run with You

no matter how
i want them to

so i'm asking You
to love me

cause i doubt
You'll ever fail

80

it started with a rumbling
working its way up from the floor
through my feet and up into my legs
and soon my head was trembling
and my heart was racing
matching the rumbling of the plane
as it sped across the tarmac
and towards something uncertain

something filled my soul
as sun filtered through the window and streaked
across my legs
i held my hand out and through the window
i could see glimpses of trees and houses as we flew up
tilting tilting tilting
scared we'd plunge down and crash

but we leveled out and now all i could
see was white beyond the window
pure white like heaven
the clouds were
the only things i could see of earth and
that made me thrilled
there is no tie

between earth and i

and i am free

81

there are colours

scattered

on my bedroom floor
and a stuffed bear
against the wall
that i've had
for half a year

lattice light
patterns the floor

i wish it could pattern
my life

perhaps it could
take away
the ache

in my head

82

there are two types of rain

hard rain
and soft rain

soft rain is memories

it's holding hands

it's a warm embrace

it's long lonely walks
pouring out your heart
to the sky as the rain
races your tears
down your cheeks

it's sad songs and loneliness
and springtime and nostalgia

hard rain

is harsher

it's anger
and arguments and fury
and dousing sluicing pain

it's sobbing in fear and screaming
in panic
and heartache

it's the loss of one knit into your very soul

it's the sharp rocks
at the foot of a cliff

it's the dread in the back of your mind
that says to listen
before it ends

83

i'm sorry
i'm not typical

i'm sorry
i'm confusing

i wish i wasn't
too much for you
or was i too little?

i'm sorry
i'm so indecisive

i'm sorry
i'm not perfect
or pretty like other girls

i'm sorry
you didn't want me

84

each breath
lasts a millisecond longer
than the one before
and my eyes
are trying to close
against the chaos
in front of me

maybe learning you
would let me understand
what it is
i'm missing

or maybe you'd see
just how selfish
i am
if you ever bothered to
learn me back

and i'm sure
you don't care
not about me anyway
and if i'm right
please don't trick me
into thinking you do
unless
you're confused
too

85

they walk
hand in hand
along the road
oblivious to it all
only looking at each other
staring into each
other's eyes
a tiny family of
two and a half
and inside my soul
i feel a twinge of happiness
like a sip of tea
on a rainy day
or a footprint
in clean crystal snow
a brick wall over grown
with ivy and nostalgia
soft green grass
under bare toes
and i smile

86

the sky weeps
salty tears
and the soil
recieves them

as a gift

from one sibling
to another

graceful clouds
sweep the
harsh
blue
sky

and despair
quakes the earth

the mountains
ache and ache
waiting
for the reconciliation

// broken world

87

" a gracious woman
retains honor "
but how can one like me
be gracious
when one like me
is a little aching
a little hurting

a mosaic
of missing
broken fairytales
that lost all hint
of grace
to the hurricane
that shattered me a little

one like me
whose heart is a little harder
sharper
older
no
please no

i want this cold
to leave
and warmth to return
let grace run home
may this everlasting echo
be evanescent again

let this soul
be soft
and bruised
and crooked
but

do not

let it become anything less
than gracious

88

i saw you
from out of the corner
of my weary eye
and all i wanted
was for you
to see me too
but i'm afraid you didn't

maybe you missed me
or maybe you caught a glance
of me
but you didn't look at me twice

maybe now i've lost the chance
i never had
but always wanted

maybe you cared
and maybe i just couldn't tell

maybe you spoke
and maybe i attached
more / less
meaning
than you meant it
to ever hold
and if that's the case
then i'm sorry

and i don't expect you
to care
but oh heavens
it would be heavenly
if you did

89

the city skyline
is built of power
and determination
both of which
tend to scare me
but glass panes
and steel
form
jagged diamonds
that will never fade
from the memory
stuck in my head

90

let me never
slip
from the truths
that i've always
clung to

becoming sea foam at the mercy
of the sea
or a marionette
controlled by
this world

i want my heart
to be as
steadfast
as the silver moon
in december
and if
i sway in the breeze

let me stay true
to what i
believe in

91

don't you dare give up
you have so much left
to live for

it sounds cliche

believe me

i know

but while you are here
you are meant to be here

perhaps this is the time for which
you were created

perhaps if you keep on breathing
you'll find your love soon
you'll find your rhythm
the path laid in front of you

perhaps a few more days
of pain and hurt
will bring about tears
of joy

don't take your life
while you're needed here

// for any soul who is aching and hurting

92

don't let
a lack of words

or

a lack of words that
fit together
dim the heart inside you

don't let an inch
of feeling fade

don't you dare
let your fire
go out

93

maybe one day
i'll put down my pen
slip into the darkness
learn things i needed
to know
but didn't

maybe i'll fall
beneath my bed
and dream
about long-lost
memories

maybe i'll swim
beyond what i've seen
beyond the rocks
of the craggy coast
in my head
and see things
i've only dreamt about

i just have one question:
will i survive
the wreckage
of my head?

94

when i was young
there was an alley
behind my home
made of laughter
and tears

an alley paved in dark cement
like the storm clouds
i fell in love with

rain would fall
and i would walk

sluicing through
the puddles that gathered
down the center
of the alley

and i would cover my feet
in rainwater

even now
i find comfort
in stinging
freezing
rain
and hard
cold
pavement

95

people fascinate me

each of us little ones

with our own stories
our own memories
our own fears
fears we have for a reason

each of us with words that
have haunted us all our lives

each of us with visions of happ`y
that we're still looking for

we each of us bear inside
a hole
that grows as we grow
filled with people we have known
and memorized
and released to go their own ways
like butterflies migrating to their destinies
a hole that is
broken
cracked
shattered
with the weight of the heartbreak
that comes from opening our souls
to be known

and

inevitably

to be hurt and torn and ripped

a hole that can only heal
if you pour out more love
more hope

more resistance against the cold
unfeeling darkness

96

she's a graceful tangle
of hope and poetry
a twisted strand
of dreaming and wisdom
a soft tapestry
of power and kindness

// for danaya

97

and if you find me
treat me gently

for i am bruised
and aching

at the pain inside
today

if you find me
let the stars sleep

in my eyes
until dawn comes again

let the moon bathe my skin
until i'm lost in the darkness

98

you were a picture
of grace in pain
a shimmering image
of strength

you laughed
and love
poured from your eyes

and forgiveness
flowed from
your hands

// for clementina

99

i used to have soft hands

hands not used to hard work
not used to being rubbed raw

i had hands that thought
love was easy
and hate hard

i had little niave hands
without a story of their own

i had hands
that believed that everyone
was good

i had hands
that held the stars

they're cracked now
they're bleeding
they're heavy
with all the pain they
have held

they're weighed down
by memories
of things i said that hurt people

they're cold
because their love
is gone

they thought
they would only love one person
but as one increased
to two and two
to four and four
to eight
their heartache grew exponentially
now they're bruised
and hurting

they're hurting with
the pain of waking up
and trying to
love again

and again

and again

they used to think
that love would
wipe out everything
and it does

but what is hidden behind
the love
if it's strong enough
will rear its ugly head again
one day
when love has grown
a little weaker

my hands thought they were brave

but they were just inexperienced

100

i wander
in my mind
combing through
forgotten dreams
and dusty ambitions

and i recall the
ache i felt
when my heart
got a little
bruised

and the fear
of growing up
overflowed from inside me

and the importance of
getting older
once again railed
at the back of my mind
and i remember
what i felt when
i learned how
to breathe again

and i catch
between my fingertips
the love
i could hand to others

and i hang on

i hang on

i hang on

and i will try
to never
let go

thank you. thank you for picking up my poetry, and reading it. i hope something touches your soul, and maybe even helps you to deal with something, for that's why i've written each of these words. thank you for being a radiant being on this earth.

thank you, my Father and my God. You are the One who has inspired these words, and any good they do anyone was worked by Your hand. thank you for constantly holding me close to Your heart, and for never letting me go. i love You.

thank you, mom and dad, for encouraging me, and supporting me. for giving me your time and your wisdom. for loving me when i'm most unlovable.

thank you, auntie marta, for publishing this little book, and for your constant support and love.

thank you, danaya, mikaela, heidi, bailey, lauren, clementina, ashley, laurel, eden, naomi, and all the other friends of mine who have loved me through this entire process. i love you all so very very very much <3 <3 <3

-daelynn

daelynn {dedh}

daelynn is a young woman from canada, and living in texas with her parents and younger siblings.

she loves poetry {life, really}, the love for other people that exists on this earth, dried flowers, old books, imagine dragons, owl city, and any books by madeleine l'engle.

www.justdilly.com
instagram.com/ dillelisadawn

www.ingramcontent.com/pod-product-compliance
Lightning Source LLC
Chambersburg PA
CBHW071500070426
42452CB00041B/1979